Guess What

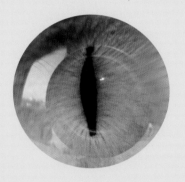

CHERRY LAKE
Publishing

Published in the United States of America by
Cherry Lake Publishing
Ann Arbor, Michigan
www.cherrylakepublishing.com

Reading Adviser: Marla Conn MS, Ed., Literacy specialist, Read-Ability, Inc.
Book Designer: Felicia Macheske

Photo Credits: © Dr.Margorius/Shutterstock.com, cover; © Africa Studio/Shutterstock.com, 1, 4; © Kuttelvaserova Stuchelova/
Shutterstock.com, 3; © schankz,/Shutterstock.com, 7, 12; © Nailia Schwarz/Shutterstock.com, 8; © Pavel Hlystov/Shutterstock.
com, 11; © Dmitrydesign/Shutterstock.com, 15; © kuban_girl/Shutterstock.com, 16; © dilynn/Shutterstock.com, 19; © Kalmatsuy/
Shutterstock.com, 21; © Andrey_Kuzmin/Shutterstock.com, back cover; © Eric Isselee/Shutterstock.com, back cover; © Andrey_
Kuzmin/Shutterstock.com, back cover

Library of Congress Cataloging-in-Publication Data

Names: Macheske, Felicia, author.
Title: Pouncing pals : cat / Felicia Macheske.
Description: Ann Arbor : Cherry Lake Publishing, [2017] | Series: Guess what
 | Audience: K to grade 3. | Includes index.
Identifiers: LCCN 2016057049| ISBN 9781634728508 (hardcover)
 | ISBN 9781534100282 (paperback) | ISBN 9781634729390 (pdf) | ISBN 9781634101173
 (hosted ebook)
Subjects: LCSH: Cats—Juvenile literature.
Classification: LCC SF445.7 .M23 2017 | DDC 636.8—dc23
LC record available at https://lccn.loc.gov/2016057049

Cherry Lake Publishing would like to acknowledge the work of The Partnership for 21st Century Skills.
Please visit *www.p21.org* for more information.

Printed in the United States of America
Corporate Graphics

Table of Contents

I can see in the dark.

My ears are shaped like triangles.

I can smell very well.

I have
soft fur.

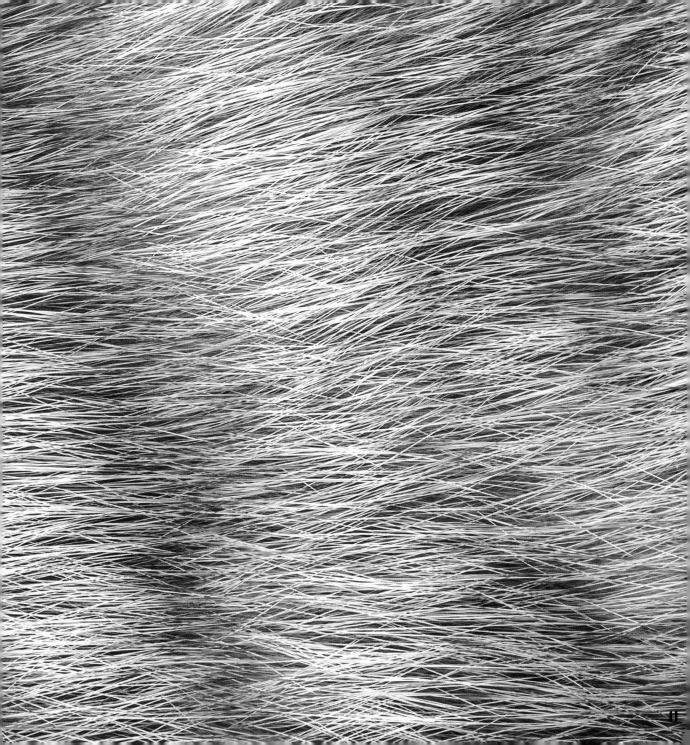

I have sharp fangs.

I use my tongue to stay clean.

I like to sharpen my claws.

I nap
a lot.

Do you know what I am?

I'm a Cat!

About Cats

1. Cats can live about 15 years.

2. There are many different colors, sizes, and shapes of cats.

3. Cats are carnivores. This means they eat mostly meat.

4. Cats use their tails to **balance**.

5. Cats spend most of their time napping.

Things to Think About
Before You Get a Pet

1. Can you take care of a pet for its whole life?

2. Do you have the money and the time to care for a pet?

3. Could you **adopt** a pet from a **rescue shelter**?

4. Do you have space in your home for a pet?

5. Can you keep a pet safe?

6. Can you keep other animals and people safe from a pet?

Glossary

adopt (uh-DOHPT) to bring an animal into your family

balance (BAL-uhns) to stay firmly fixed and not shaky

fangs (FANGZ) an animal's long, pointed teeth

rescue shelter (RES-kyoo SHEL-tur) a place where an animal that was in danger or was not wanted can stay

smell (SMEL) to sense an odor with your nose

Index